Leaves of Light and Silent Fire

ENGLISH EDITION

Leaves of Light and Silent Fire

ENGLISH EDITION

ENNIS M. SALAM

Copyright © 2025 Ennis M. Salam

All rights reserved

ISBN: 979-8-3132-3440-3

A NOTE ON THE ENGLISH EDITION

This English-language edition of Leaves of Light and Silent Fire *is presented as a prelude to the forthcoming complete bilingual edition. Due to current publishing limitations with Amazon Kindle Direct Publishing, which preclude the inclusion of Arabic script, the original Arabic poems have been temporarily omitted. This edition allows me to share my work with you — my friends and admirers — without further delay.*

The complete bilingual edition, honoring the elegance and richness of both English and Arabic verses, is forthcoming, encompassing the full depth of my creative vision.

With gratitude for your understanding and anticipation for what lies ahead,

Ennis M. Salam

*For my little brother, Omar,
Teo, and M.W.*

ACKNOWLEDGEMENTS

I extend my profound gratitude to Michael Hatcher, Jasmine Games, and the every.Word Poetry platform: their open mics were my creative sanctuary. Michael's unwavering belief in my voice guided me toward assembling these poems into a single, cohesive collection.

A special tribute to my brother, Rad—an exquisite poet, a guiding mentor, and a living testament to compassion's transformative power.

CONTENTS

LOVE OF FAMILY	1
LOVE OF FRIENDS	22
LOVE OF ROMANCE	45
LOVE OF LIFE	105

LOVE OF FAMILY

AUTUMN LEAVES IN THE LONG NIGHT OF WAR

Beirut weeps, the south bleeds wounds that won't heal
Voices rise in the sky, like screams of pain they peel
Ships unleash their fires, missiles fall like heavy rain
Our family scatters like autumn leaves in night's domain

Grandmother left to Jordan, carrying nostalgia in her eyes
My aunt weeps for a homeland, a home wounded by lies
Relatives from the south fill our small abode
Six souls seeking safety on this perilous road

The noise of jets and shields breaks the dark night's peace
I call my brother: "Good morning, you mischievous piece!"
He laughs and says: "Life's a movie, and we are the cast"
But his eyes tell of sorrow, wounds that ever last

I try to make him forget the pain with jokes and talk
I send him about the perils of smoke and the path we walk
He says: "Why live so long in a world like this?"
Yet his heart beats with life, amid the abyss

WHISPERS OF PEACE AMIDST THE SMOKE

Each morning, I call to you through clouds of smoke
My voice slips between bombs, reaching you like a whisper of peace
I laugh with you, speaking as the breeze speaks to the flowers
We live amidst the world's clamor, like two birds fluttering in fierce winds

You mock the smoke, saying: "Perhaps life can be shortened"
And I laugh, but my heart whispers: "Don't let your light fade, my hero"
I don't fear for your life, but I fear life will carry you far away
That you'll be lost like so many others, with hope slipping from your hands

We talk like waves speak to the sea, endlessly
Words carry us far from the war, painting poems in the sky
You are not just a cousin, you are a star in the sky of my life
And as bombs fall, we remain standing, lighting the night with laughter and love

A FLOWER OF HOPE BENEATH THE RUBBLE

In a city that sleeps upon the shoulders of sea and mountains
A girl carries in her heart the light of morning and ambitions
From a humble family, yet her aspirations reach the sky
I helped her achieve her dream, to step towards the high

Accepted into the university of light, knowledge, and grandeur
She begins her journey in a world of thought and wonder
But fate had another opinion on the path she'd chart
A missile fell, destroyed her home, tore her world apart

She and her family fled, carrying nothing but their attire
Left homeless, amidst pain and a world on fire
Yet her spirit remains strong, like a flower in the breeze
Facing storms, she shines, her smile brings us ease

LEMON REVERIE: CHILDHOOD DREAMS AND TALES OF ETERNITY

Do you remember, my brother, the city balcony?
Where we sat together under the evening sun,
Our grandfather bringing baskets of golden lemons,
We'd eat them until our tongues burned with life's longing.

We devoured lemons whole, with their peels, smiling,
Throwing the rinds at the passersby below,
Our laughter rose above the noise,
The innocence of our childhood filling the air with joy.

In the mountain house, we'd run to the orchard,
Climbing the high branches of lemon trees,
Picking fruits with our small hands,
Filling our pockets with the earth's treasures.

The tree branches embraced us,
The wind sang us songs of freedom,
We gazed at the distant horizon,
Dreaming of a world without end.

We carried the rugs outside, shaking off the dust,
Sprinkling water on the stone courtyards,
Washing the ground as we cleansed our hearts,
Reviving the silent corners of the house.

Our fatigue was mixed with love,
Every corner told a story,
As if we wove threads of memories,
In the fabric of unforgettable time

And today, my brother, under a shattered sky,
I hear in your voice the echo of bombs,
Jets breaking the sound barrier,
Smoke covering our old balcony.

Yet your heart still carries the light,
You are the tree that doesn't bend,
Your roots delve into the land of our ancestors,
Your branches embrace the sky of hope.

In your eyes, I see a homeland that doesn't die,
We are the children of lemons and soil,
We will climb the trees and laugh again,
And rebuild what has been destroyed.

My brother, you are the note that defies silence,
The dream that refuses to break,
Together we will write new chapters,
In the story of life and resilience.

CEDARS OF DUSK: THE SILENCE OF THE EIGHT HOUR

On a night when the sky is falling, crumbling down
The enemy hastens steps, fires burn the ground
Trying to hit everything before time runs out at eight
I'm sitting on my nerves, awaiting the destined date

Shelling intensifies, the sky rains fire and woe
My brother sends: "Bombs are falling like the snow"
The university closed, displaced fill every space
Children cry in fear, mothers in a desperate place

Eight o'clock approaches, I count seconds in despair
Will this madness cease, or continue without care?
My brother says: "The enemy tries to destroy every place"
I pray to God with fervor, for peace to fill our space

When the clock struck eight, the world paused for a while
Planes still hovered, but shelling ceased its trial
My brother says: "Perhaps this violent war has ceased"
We rejoiced cautiously, our joy was mild at least

Our city lies in ruins, destruction all around
Where will the homeless go? How to rebuild the ground?
We carry hope within us, despite the pain and scars
And we'll start anew, no matter how tough things are

NOBLE EMBER

A pillar in our home, you stood unwavering,
Rooted in the memories of a homeland torn by war.
I speak of the nights you spent reciting verses
While your heart throbbed with longing for lost family.

You traversed the harsh roads of Europe,
Facing the glare of indifference, the lure of dark alleys,
Yet you clung to the light of faith
Like a sailor guided by the North Star.

In the States, you found neither ease nor luxury at first—
Only the promise of tomorrow's bread
Earned by the sweat of your brow.
But you molded that promise into a sturdy foundation
For your children, ensuring we grew up
In the embrace of religion and the melody of Arabic.
No distance could break the ties to Lebanon, Syria, or Iraq,
For you made sure we knew our roots,
The music of our shared lineage.

When I was ten, you sensed a spark fading in me—
Our heritage slipping away, replaced by foreign phrases
And the distractions of a world spinning too fast.
You decided we must leave America for a season,
Sacrificing your own comfort, your marriage's peace,
All to seal our bond with faith and family.
Qatar became our classroom,
Our hearts the slate on which you inscribed
The verses of devotion and belonging.

But enough of speaking *about* you—
Now I face you, Father, across the distance of years.
I recall the nights when you forbade me
From running off to chase idle play:
"Sit here," you'd say, "and listen."
Those words shaped me more than any school lesson,
Teaching me the weight of responsibility,
The breadth of knowledge found in adult discourse.
Father, I am twenty-four,
Yet in the mirror of your guidance, I see a wisdom
Carved by your unwavering hand.
Every breath I draw is tinted by your sacrifice,
Every prayer I utter is an echo of your faith.

I love you, Father.
My gratitude for you transcends language,
But I pour these verses at your feet,
Hoping they convey a fraction of my debt.
Your life, carved from the rubble of war
And polished by perseverance,
Is a testament to what the human spirit can endure.
I stand on the shore of your legacy,
Ready to sail onward with the compass
You placed gently in my palm.

HE WEARS THE ECHOS OF CEDARS

He wears the echo of cedars in his voice,
A resonance carried from Lebanon's high peaks
To the distant horizons where new beginnings await.

Seventeen years of youth overshadowed
By the thunder of war,
He journeyed across Europe's grey cities
With little more than courage in his pocket.

In each foreign street, his footsteps marked
A testament to survival,
A vow to remain unbroken
Even when roots were torn from the soil.

He arrived in America like a seed
Blown off-course by a storm,
Yet determined to flourish in strange earth.

Days blurred into nights in humble apartments,
Where faith lit the dim rooms
And gave him strength to keep going.

His children would learn to pray in Arabic
And speak the mother tongue
As if they had never left the land of their ancestors.

No sacrifice was too great for that dream,
Not even uprooting his family again
To ensure tradition thrived in the desert air of Qatar.

He, the pillar of his household,
Carried the weight of distant families on his shoulders—
Letters, calls, and unwavering concern
For relatives scattered across Lebanon, Syria, and Iraq.

Every tear shed in private
Fueled his will to protect his loved ones.
He never boasted of his trials;
He simply built a home of belonging
So his children could stand firm in the storms of life.

He wears the echo of cedars still,
A living testament to endurance and love.

LOVE OF FRIENDS

REGAL MOMENTUM

In twilight's masquerade of worldly guise,
Your eyes—luminous beacons—cut through the dark.
With sculptor's care you shape the mortal clay,
Shattering ancient chains with a fearless spark.

A bridge you form to realms beyond the known,
Where strength is forged in fires of wild, raw might.
You taught me how to kindle inner power,
And walk through every tempest toward the light.

Once lost amid despair's relentless vale,
You breathed the daring of a noble soul.
Lifting me above the muted, herd-like song,
You carved a path uniquely fierce and whole.

Your wisdom drifts upon the winds of time,
A quiet hymn that bids my spirit climb.
Each stride I take resounds with your profound grace—
A living testament to what you've magnified.

In me you see the seed of greatness sown,
A being unbound by common mortal chains.
Together we unveil life's veiled pretense,
Embracing all its wild and wondrous strains.

In the crucible of pain our art is born,
Transforming suffering into fierce rebirth.
Like a phoenix rising from cleansing flame,
I mirror your resolve across the earth.

Our souls, unbound by ordinary ties,
Engage in an eternal, daring dance.
Within you echoes of recurrence sing—
Two sovereign lights, each holding its expanse.

ANCHOR IN THE TEMPEST'S EMBRACE

Deep in the garden of my inner night,
A fragile seed was sown by gentle hands—
Hands that knew the secret language of the earth
And nurtured life with unseen, sacred plans.

You are the sun that warms my dormant clay,
The steadfast moon to guide me through the dark.
A mirror in which my hidden self appears,
In your embrace I find my vital spark.

I wandered, lone and lost, in midnight's thrall,
Till your soft light unveiled a hopeful path.
Amidst the storm's relentless, surging roar,
Your patience anchored me in love's warm bath.

When I strayed, your tears fell like healing rain,
A stream that washed away each creeping doubt.
In silent words our hearts conspired as one—
A language only kindred souls speak out.

O mentor, guide, and father of my days,
Your wisdom lights the way to brighter dawns.
Each lesson glows with love's enduring fire,
A tapestry of hope forever drawn.

I offer now the fruit of my ascent,
A humble pledge born of devoted care.
In striving to embody all you are,
I honor you—my north, my constant prayer.

Together, like a timeless cosmic song,
We sing a harmony that will not fade.
In you I see the timeless truth of friendship,
A bond that forever shall our hearts pervade.

So let us waltz through sacred, endless space,
Two souls conjoined in life's eternal grace.
With your strong hand to guide me on the way,
I journey where our spirits soar and stay.

THE LUMINOUS ATELIER

Between exile's edge and the warmth of home,
I wandered in shadows, longing yet to roam;
Your gentle hand reached through my darkest night,
And built within my heart a haven of light.

You are an ancient olive, steadfast and wise,
A guide beneath the ever-stretching skies;
I am the branch that yearns for your embrace,
Finding in your strength a constant, tender grace.

Across the pages of time your verses gleam,
Crafting dreams of courage like a steadfast beam;
Your voice, a compass leading ever true,
Unveils fresh paths to worlds I never knew.

I pledge to learn and grow with fervent fire,
To honor every lesson that you inspire;
In your kind eyes I see both past and lore,
And futures waiting just beyond the door.

Together we tread where old and new combine,
Your measured steps align my own in time;
Each stone we raise becomes a pillar strong,
A monument to love that rights all wrong.

When silence falls upon a crowded street,
Your words revive my pulse with steady beat;
A shared rhythm sings of hope so deep and clear,
A whispered promise that you'll always be near.

You are the poet of my silent cries,
The dawn that breaks the longest, bleakest skies;
Within you dwell the verses yet unsung,
A timeless language spoken by the young.

Let these verses form our everlasting bridge,
Uniting every gain and loss upon life's ridge;
Together, side by side, our story we recite,
A sacred bond reborn in love's resplendent light.

CELESTIAL COUTURE

In life's vast tapestry our threads entwine,
Your soul interlaced so seamlessly with mine;
No force can sever where our spirits reside,
United in purpose, our hearts walk side by side.

You are the echo of my most profound call,
Lifting me high whenever I begin to fall;
In the mirror of my heart your face appears,
A boundless sea of truth that steadily clears.

Through you, the world's deep mysteries take flight,
Ancient lore and secrets glow with radiant light;
You lead me to a well of wisdom, pure and sure,
Unlocking hidden doors with guidance that's secure.

I offer you devotion's flame so bright and rare,
A pledge unending, crafted with the utmost care;
Together we strive to shape a nobler art,
Kindling love's immortal fire within each heart.

You name the essence behind each veiling guise,
Revealing truths where falsehood dares to rise;
In every grain of sand the cosmos sings,
And every breath renews the hope that freedom brings.

Our hearts converse in silence, deep and clear,
A union where true meaning always draws near;
You serve as my compass, ever true and right,
Illuminating all my paths with steadfast light.

In the garden of our souls we walk as friends,
On journeys that have neither start nor end;
Our bond, eternal, radiates a gentle air,
A timeless testament beyond all compare.

May our story echo as a cherished rhyme,
A hymn of souls transcending bounds of time;
Together we rise, our spirits soaring high above,
Embarking on an endless flight of wings and love.

THE PATIENCE OF PRESTIGE

In the city of the soul where dreams take flight,
You stand as architect, a beacon burning bright;
A master craftsman shaping wandering clay,
Molding a path where virtue lights the way.

A sage whose wisdom warms the cloak of night,
Kindling reason's flame with insights pure and light;
With careful art, you weave both truth and art,
A tapestry where ethics rest within the heart.

I rise, an eager pupil, to your noble call,
Embracing vast knowledge that you gently install;
Each step toward my best self becomes my due,
A living tribute to the legacy of you.

In deep discourse we search for what is real,
Exploring ancient realms with a modern zeal;
Your thoughtful questions stir convictions anew,
Nurturing the soil where my deepest truths grew.

Together we pursue the highest good we know,
In justice, courage, and the dreams that ever glow;
You reveal the city thriving in each soul,
Where harmony and light together make us whole.

Each step we ascend is cherished like a gift,
Lifting our hopes and giving tired hearts a lift;
In our united quest for all that is right,
We chase the ever-glowing beacon through the night.

Your patience is the fertile soil from which I bloom,
My roots run deep in truths that ever shall resume;
As branches reach up to caress the endless skies,
They drink the wisdom your tender guidance supplies.

In our profound bond the highest ideals come alive,
Reflecting life's grand design, helping us survive;
Together we build a timeless, sacred art,
A fellowship of souls forever joined in heart.

DAWN OF THE VANGUARD

At 7:45, while the city still dreams,
We meet at Teo's where raw energy teems.
Weights clang in cadence as muscles strain,
In dawn's gentle blush, we shatter each chain.

Cappy's bright laughter cascades through the air,
While Rad's robust power shines bold and rare.
C spins his tales to illuminate our way,
And Lou's stately presence is here to stay.

Teo commands with poise—a beacon so grand,
While Doug's sage insights help us firmly stand.
Each rep we execute lifts our souls on high,
United we soar beneath the awakening sky.

When the sweat of our efforts gives hunger a call,
We escape to Desudo's, where fine coffee enthralls.
Veracruz tacos—a savory art on display—
Reignite our fire to embrace the next play.

At Lou's, we reconvene as one refined crew,
Wim Hof's deep breaths renew our strength anew.
With fire and ice, we boldly dare to chase,
Within the sauna's heat, we each find our space.

Heart to heart, our inner secrets congeal,
In that fervid heat, our cherished truths reveal.
In life's crucible, our narratives blend,
As wisdom and kinship forge bonds without end.

At twenty-four, I stand 'mid giants so bold,
Their silent triumphs like treasures of old.
I absorb each lesson as a devoted acolyte,
Their mentorship guiding me through the night.

Each Saturday, our sacred rite we keep,
A brotherhood of souls, unyieldingly deep.
Every week unfolds a vibrant, fresh art—
With gratitude, I enshrine this collective heart.

VELVET LIBERATION

Among the many souls who wept while I stood cold and proud,
My mask held firm as others' cries and sorrows screamed aloud.
I bore my trauma's legacy, as silent as the stone,
And found some power in that hush, a kingdom of my own.

Then David, with no sharpened sword, struck at my guarded core,
He wrested truth from iron limbs I'd sealed behind the door.
My lips, once mute and measured, hurled a furious, raw decree:
"Fuck you!" I cried with trembling rage, and fists of plea.

O shame, how swift your burden fell upon my shattered frame,
As tears I deemed forever lost now struggled into flame.
In yielding to the breaking tide, I tasted pain and grace,
For what once was numbness fled before compassion's face.

Now, I salute the one who dared to wound my silent art,
To tear the veil that pride had sown around my wounded heart.
I love you, David, for the gift of truth no mask could hide,
Through your calm stance, I learn to feel, unarmoured, open wide.

NOCTURNE OF THE UNBOUND

Alyssa, I stepped into this room with armour bright and tall,
Convinced that all my pains were tamed behind a mighty wall.
Others wept with open hearts as hours stretched so long,
While I stood cold and wondering why their tears felt wrong.

You cried, "What do you want?" until your voice was all I knew,
I offered distant words—connection!—but it did not ring true.
In my mind, a father's silence stood where I could not tread,
Though I've danced with strangers easily, my love for him lay dead.

How can a stranger's soul embrace what I so freely give,
While with my father's guarded face, I barely learn to live?
A woman has shared her tender home, tears of love were mine,
Yet my father's heart stays distant, dim, and undefined.

Your question held a mirror to the fear I kept inside,
My eyes filled up with salted truth that I could never hide.
Your voice, Alyssa, pried apart the barriers I'd raised,
And made me see the hollow rooms where fragile longing grazed.

Alyssa, in that moment's cry, my fortress fell at last,
Your words became a bridge to what I'd long held in the past.
I thank your daring honesty, the way you made me see,
That healing comes in strangers' tears, setting my own heart free.

LIGHT OF MY EYE

I measured your dreams with my own faint measure,
And doubted your growth while chasing my pleasure.
But sorrow now seeps wherever I roam,
I beg for your pardon to brighten my home.

I called you too humble, too gentle your art,
Ignoring the music that played in your heart.
Yet wisdom now shows me how wrong was my fear,
Your brilliance shone softly, so precious and clear.

In the orchard of souls, each blossom must rise,
No dream is too small beneath boundless skies.
I bow in contrition, my voice trembling low,
Your purpose deserves every chance it can grow.

To label your calling with casual scorn
Was forging a darkness where doubt could be born.
But from these gray ashes compassion will gleam,
I learn from your vision and honor your dream.

The soul is a treasure no scale can define,
No title too modest for spirit divine.
Your coaching illuminates hearts in the night,
A torch in the silence, a guiding delight.

Forgive me, dear friend, if I tarnished your grace,
My own timid mirrors obscured your bright face.
For love is a realm where we see and unite,
Together, more radiant, we share the same light.

Compassion now flowers in each word I say,
I cherish your mission, no matter the way.
As Rumi once taught, we are candles of love,
We shine all the brighter when lit from above.

Receive this contrition, a penitent plea,
I stand here awakened, more humble, and free.
Your dream is a jewel that ever must glow,
And I, now enlightened, will help it to grow.

BEAT OF MY HEART

I spoke like a thunder, my verses were grand,
Yet deaf to your dream and the hope in your hand.
My pride was a fortress, I deemed you too small,
But in wounding your spirit, I stumbled and fell.

I mocked your ambition, your vision so pure,
Blind to the gold in a heart that is sure.
Now shame is my guest, how it gnaws at my core,
A poet undone by a fault I deplore.

A coach, I belittled, as if less than might,
Yet stars that are hidden still shine in the night.
No calling is minor when forged by the soul,
No crown is more radiant than one that is whole.

So, humbled, I stand at the door of your grace,
To seek your forgiveness, to heal this displaced.
My words, once a weapon, I soften with care,
And hope you can trust what these new verses bear.

Forgive my ambition that soared without end,
I missed the true power that lies in a friend.
Your path may be smaller in name or in view,
But it blossoms with purpose, ignited by you.

Let not my misjudgment eclipse what we share,
In your gentle guidance, there's comfort so rare.
A coach's compassion can crown human hearts,
And that is the grandest of all royal arts.

I offer these lines as my olive branch true,
The poet in me bows in reverence to you.
With words steeped in truth, I uphold your flame,
No longer I scorn but give honor and name.

May wounds of the past now be graced by the sun,
Let friendship arise when our shadows are done.
Your dream is a mountain that climbs through the sky,
And I shall stand by you, in hope lifted high.

LOVE OF ROMANCE

*I have danced with over a thousand women,
and you are by far the best.*

SARAH CONNOR

In White Horse we danced a daring two-step,
Where glances intertwined and two hearts leapt.
At first, I paused at the taste of a kiss so sweet,
Afraid to rob the stars of their shimmering seat.

Under the trees in our second refrain,
In the car we loved until dawn could reign.
Our heads spilled outside through that open door,
Embracing magic we'd never known before.

You left a gentle mark on my thumb,
On my back, your ardent traces clung.
In moments of madness I cried "Ay Ya Yay,"
And you laughed—your eyes lit as sparks in the fray.

Five hours vanished like seconds in flight,
While leaves sang our story deep into the night.
No one existed but you and me,
A world we forged from a glance and a key.

We marveled at the onlookers' curious delight,
How desire is stoked by each envious sight.
On the third night, a farewell and a gift,
I offered my heart and secrets adrift.

Your lips were sweeter than sugar's grace,
A taste that melted my soul into place.

Don't change that smile, or who you are,
Remain your wondrous, unaltered star.
You're the only one in that fourth tier,
A secret we share, understood without fear.

HALOS OF METAL AT THE WITCHING HOUR

In hidden corners few dare roam,
We carved a world where we were alone.
Your hair, a silver thread of moonlight,
A leopard skirt in the hush of night.

A belt of bullets resting at your side,
Whispers of journeys we'd never tried.
"Why fix your hair?" I teased with ease,
"No one exists but you and me."

We drank leftover spirits found in cans,
Glasses half-full like contraband.
A shared cigarette, hush thick in the air,
Smoke like vows we were too bold to spare.

Your camera sought a glimmer of truth,
Yet couldn't capture our fleeting youth.
Moments lived outside any frame,
Memories dear, unnamed by name.

Beneath the sky's star-braided dome,
I poured my drink upon the loam.
To taste your lips—a sacred quest,
In that kiss, our souls confessed.

A lime, tangy, between us shared,
You took it from my lips, unprepared.
In that fearless act, the world withdrew,
No witness but the shadows—and we two.

"Who cares who's watching?" we silently agreed,
In that universe, only us we did heed.
Wrapped in darkness, free of sight,
We owned the world in that sacred night.

DELIRIUM IN LILAC DAYBREAK

On a tranquil night beneath the moon's soft grace,
She slept upon my chest in a peaceful place.
Our heads brushed whispers of the open sky,
Feet reaching where horizons lie.

I kissed each finger, slow and deep,
A secret vow the night would keep.
We spent long hours in hush and hold,
Until our lips, by passion, grew cold.

With a hidden smile, I whispered low,
"Our lips are dry," but you let me know,
"Come closer, let me quench that fire,"
Your nectar poured with gentle desire.

A leftover lime between my teeth,
You claimed with a kiss, warm beneath.
From my taste to yours the flavor streamed,
Where souls and senses truly gleamed.

At dawn, birds sang in joyful tune,
Leaves danced around us in bright commune.
Never before have I felt such calm,
As though we drifted in a dream's sweet palm.

No one but us in this woven sphere,
The present alive, the future unclear.
For love stands tall as our shining decree,
A poem unending in you and me.

OVERTURE OF THE UNFORSEEN

Like morning dew that crowns the dawn,
You appeared, then suddenly you were gone.
But in that flash, the world stood still,
A chalice of emotion we chose to fill.

No moral shade, no past to mend,
Just pure connection without an end.
They say brief flames burn to fade,
But ours left a warmth that wouldn't evade.

When I spoke and you came near,
Your tightened grasp made intention clear.
Unclouded minds, hearts stripped of fear,
A realm of truth—nothing more dear.

Perhaps the brevity made it pure,
A rare essence, shining and sure.
Though time was short, and roads diverged,
Its impact remains, forever emerged.

Yet guilt sometimes wraps its chain,
For feeling peace while you abstain.
I wonder how it can be so,
Should letting go become my woe?

CELESTIAL WALTZ

In the muted echoes of a waning tune,
I wander alone beneath a spectral moon.
At White Horse, we danced in perfect rhyme,
Our hearts attuned beyond the bounds of time.

You burned—a flame of unbridled desire,
A leather muse, your gaze set all afire.
We sipped on Jameson's amber, liquid art,
While your laughter banished darkness from my heart.

Now the dance floor lies cold in silent space,
Bereft of your spark and untamed grace.
Regret murmurs softly with each fading call,
A tapestry woven of both rise and fall.

A gentle breeze ushers a transient embrace,
Like a ballerina's poise, an angel's grace.
We shared a cigarette beneath the jeweled skies,
Yet that tender presence failed to still my sighs.

Still, something vital is missing—a fiery flare,
The vibrant rhythm we once boldly did share.
She drifts like a whisper—delicate, slight,
Yet fails to ignite my soul's inner light.

Oh, restless heart, why cradle this deep ache,
When even sorrow longs for solace's sake?
Is love but a dance of fleeting, transient chance,
A murmured vow within a brief romance?

I return to where our footsteps first aligned,
But joy eludes me, lost in what I cannot find.
The warmth of whiskey, the cadence of the flow,
Your silent wink remains an echo long ago.

Perhaps by clinging to shadows, I keep you near,
A cherished refrain whispered soft and clear.
Though new melodies now fill the quiet space,
Your enduring song time cannot displace.

Let the winds bear forth this wistful, tender sigh,
A tribute to a bond that shall not die.
For every dance etched upon the soul's expanse
Leaves us yearning—and yet, somehow, complete in its trance.

RAINSONG IN AN ABANDONED MEADOW

Beneath a weeping sky, I stand,
Among the ruins of my thoughts,
The laughter of a child afar,
Reminds me of the joy you've brought.

A celebration left behind,
I wander to an empty field,
With every sip and smoky breath,
Old wounds begin to gently yield.

The fallen log becomes my throne,
As tears carve rivers down my face,
A heartfelt cry for beauty lost,
For moments time cannot erase.

Your image dances in my mind,
Leopard skirt and eyes ablaze,
We spun like whispers in the night,
Now lost within this autumn haze.

I lay upon the hill's embrace,
The earth and I become as one,
The clouds, they churn like restless hearts,
A mirror of what's come undone.

Rain kisses softly on my skin,
A baptism of grief and hope,
I seek shelter in memories,
To find the strength that helps me cope.

Returning to my lone retreat,
The hatchback open to the storm,
I close my eyes and hear your voice,
A phantom touch that once was warm.

Is it the person or the time,
That haunts the corridors of me?
Perhaps they're threads of the same line,
Woven into eternity.

HINTERLAND OF MIRAGE AND EMBER

I linger at the crossroads of emotion,
A wanderer trapped between two sands.
One desert is the mirage of infatuation,
The other, an oasis where true love stands.

Your image, etched upon the prowling wind,
A fleeting silhouette across the sun.
Is it love that summons me near,
Or just the thrill of a race half-run?

We shared nights like stolen art,
Passion etched on an endless canvas.
Yet morning awakens doubts in my heart:
Is this our future, or something that can't last?

Infatuation is a restless guest,
Knocking but never staying for tea.
Love, instead, builds a secret nest,
A refuge where souls roam free.

I trace your face in absent memory,
Hoping to find truth in your unseen eyes.
Is this devotion or longing's tapestry,
Or echoes that lonely breath implies?

Perhaps we're travelers lost in time,
Our paths crossing just to drift apart.
Yet in the hallways of my mind,
You make a home inside my heart.

So speak, O wind that carries her away,
Does she ponder the same divide?
Between infatuation's sudden foray,
And love's steadfast, eternal tide?

DUSK-PRAYER OF THE ROOTLESS HEART

Beneath a canopy of restless stars,
I stand alone on this silent rise.
"Wind," I call, "you who wander afar,
Where do her tender feelings lie?"

"You've danced amid her silken hair,
Have you caught the secrets floating there?
Does she recall our midnight ties,
Or let those memories pass her by?"

Is it love that seeds this restless thirst,
Or infatuation's fleeting burst?
Am I a name she can't recall,
A vanishing echo behind her wall?

The wind, in sorrowful notes, replies,
"I'm a traveler too beneath these skies,
Carrying bits of hearts gone astray,
Scattered like stars in the cosmic fray."

"Infatuation—a guest who leaves
Before the tea can properly steep.
Love settles in like a friend who grieves,
A vow the soul is bound to keep."

"She speaks in sighs and silent songs,
Her eyes fixed on horizons long.
Between the lines of where she belongs,
Your image lingers, sure and strong."

"But tell me, wanderer," the wind inquires,
"Is it she you love, or love's desires?
Do you chase warmth from nights long gone,
Or seek a truth you can build upon?"

I pause, the question carved in stone,
Probing places once unknown.
"Perhaps it's both," I softly speak,
"A merging tide of all I seek."

"Then let this path your spirit guide,"
The wind surrounds me, gentle, wide.
"Whether love or fleeting tide,
Your truth is something only you decide."

NOCTURNAL ÉLAN: THE MOON'S RHAPSODY

I wander beneath the hush of moonlit skies,
A solitary figure in night's disguise.
"Moon," I whisper, "you who watch from above,
Can you see the longing that I'm unsure of?"

You observe both lovers and the lonely,
Keeper of secrets, shining so calmly.
Have you glimpsed her silhouette in your glow,
Does she too release a silent woe?

Infatuation flickers like passing clouds,
Shadows that dance across your silver shrouds.
But love endures like your patient light,
Ever-present against the darkest night.

The moon replies with a gentle beam,
"I've seen hearts wax and wane in dream.
Infatuation twirls in my faint rays,
But dissolves at dawn's encroaching blaze."

"She stands upon her balcony,
Reflecting my glow in reverie.
Her thoughts, a tide that yearns for more,
Perhaps they drift to your distant shore."

"Moon," I sigh, "is this love or just desire,
A fleeting spark in midnight's fire?"
Her smile hides behind a wisp of cloud,
"Only time can prove what hearts avowed."

"Infatuation hurries on,
Leaving before the night is gone.
But love remains, an old, dear friend,
A vow we keep until life's end."

I inhale this wisdom soft and wise,
A borrowed light for searching eyes.
"Thank you, Moon," I gently say,
"For guiding me along the way."

What a shame. What a mirror.

NOCTURNAL EMBROIDERY OF LOSS

Night's hush turned warmer
A guarded kiss in the dark
Stripped our old friendship
Morning weighs on parted hearts
Silence defines what's left now

SONATA FOR A DRIFTING SOUL

We shared trust for ages
A single kiss changed our course
I withheld my heart
Fear soared louder than longing
Now she, dear love, drifts away

SHATTERED BASILICA OF PROMISE

Brave enough to touch
But not to stand beside her
Scared of what might be
That fear snapped our bond of ages
Now dreams echo in absence

THE SLEEPER AND THE SPEECHLESS

In my arms she slept
Gentle warmth I could not name
I choked on my words
Told her not to dream of us
Truth drowned beneath timid lies

HOLLOW THORNE OF HALF-MEANT PROMISES

She trusted my heart
I offered only caution
Yet I craved her touch
I almost said "Stay forever"
Too late, I stand here alone

GOSSAMER THREADS OF FORSAKEN TRUST

She looked at me, torn
I watched her faith in me fade
All for want of yes
My lie was coward's armour
Now friendship is cast aside

PHANTASM OF UNMOURNED EUPHORIA

Echoes of her laugh
Linger where we once felt safe
I locked out my need
Told her the bond meant nothing
Lies swallow me in longing

THE DIAMOND-SHAPED QUIETUS

A single teardrop
Shimmered on her silent cheek
Reflecting my face
I reached out to wipe it clean
But pride withheld the motion

THE LOST SUNRISE

I kneel to the echoes of our midnight confession,
Like a wanderer in the desert of memory,
Sifting through dunes of your laughter,
Hoping for footprints that remain.

Night's wind carried your quiet entreaty,
An egg of faith placed in my trembling hands.
I cradled it, promised it no harm,
As the breeze turned pages of our whispered stories.

In the hush of that parked car, we shed our armour,
Tears of reflection carving pathways on my face.
You gave me a glimpse of who I could become,
And I marveled at the dawn in your eyes.

Darkness yielded to a new kind of sunrise,
Hours merged from 4 AM to 6 PM in your embrace.
A homeland for two pilgrims seeking refuge,
Even as fear hovered on the edge of each breath.

Your gaze was a pair of eclipses—
When it fell upon me, I vanished into your depths.
I tasted the birth of suns on your lips,
Forgot the lonely boundaries of my world.

But the sun can be unkind to fragile things:
It exposes every hairline fracture, every hidden doubt.
I watched your warmth retreat into silence,
A silence that eclipsed the words we once treasured.

Gone is the warmth of that unspoken vow,
Gone the shared pulse of breath and beating heart.
The phone is mute, the horizon empty—
I call out, but only echoes return.

Where is that girl who placed her fragile egg in my hands?
Where is the fierce dreamer who danced in my arms?
Where is the nighttime pilgrim who guided me toward morning,
Who pulled me from slumber into awakening bliss?
Where is the partner whose eyes once ignited my hope,
Lingering on the threshold of dawn yet choosing not to enter?

THE SWORD IN MY CHEST

The blade of words I brandish bright,
Yet in my heart, there's waning light.
I promised I would guard her trust,
But fear soon ground my vow to dust.

We wore our wounds like regal gowns,
Our teardrops crowned us kings and clowns.
I longed to mend each tortured seam,
But woke to find it was a dream.

Our night stretched on from four till day,
In burning arms, I lost my way.
But fear revived at morning's crest,
My vow lay caged within my chest.

That pledge to keep her spirit clear
Lay buried by my timid fear.
Where is the girl whose light I claimed?
Why is her warmth now left untamed?

My tears exposed a guarded heart,
A fear of closeness from the start.
In half-spun truths, I was deceived,
And shattered trust she once believed.

Each whispered vow we nearly made
Has turned to ghosts I can't evade.
Her silent phone is all I hear,
The price I pay for coward's fear.

A sword remains within my chest,
Its hilt a vow I never pressed.
I held her heart within my sight,
Yet terror stole my chance at light.

To her, I said, "Don't wait for me,"
But that betrayed the truth I see.
I want her hand, yet stand alone,
My dread a fortress turned to stone.

Yet through the bruise of parted ways,
A tender hope still meets my gaze.
If only I had shown my part,
Then sunrise might have graced her heart.

So hear me now, for I have grown,
I won't forsake the chance I've blown.
I face the cost of fear so strong,
And seek the dawn where we belong.

STILLNESS WHERE DEVOTION UNRAVELED

My footprints vanish in silent sand,
Where once we walked in union grand;
You asked for truth I could not speak,
And fear left every word so weak.

Between all wisdom and desire,
My trembling spirit sparks like fire;
My children's eyes remain my light,
Yet I recall your face at night.

A friend was lost through broken vow,
I stand unsure, even now;
I'm torn by faith and longing's call,
While regretful shadows slip and fall.

What once was pure—a bond of trust,
Is now but memory and dust;
I deemed you naive, a soul so young,
And in reflection, I'm undone.

For wisdom grows a lonely spine,
And leaves the heart with less to shine;
The root of doubt entangled me,
So from your arms I had to flee.

Your ghost remains in whispered dreams,
I drown within these midnight streams;
A path not taken haunts my soul,
And leaves half-joy that's never whole.

I weigh my children's fragile hope,
While seeking gentler ways to cope;
Between devotion, fear, and need,
My heart bleeds words I dare not heed.

A friend you were beyond compare,
A comfort once so warm and rare;
I let you slip through trembling hands,
Unsure of faith's or love's demands.

The wise would say to choose what's right,
Yet still my soul craves love's delight;
I'm trapped behind these counsel bars,
Reaching for you across the stars.

I scorned your cries, so quick to judge,
In truth, my fear refused to budge;
My childish ways, I must confess,
Have wrought this tale of emptiness.

Yet in the dawn, your name I hear,
A prayer that trembles bright and clear;
If time could only backward flow,
I'd cling to all I dared not show.

Our bond was severed by a blade,
No gentle words for me to stay;
I weigh the cost of fleeting pride,
Which left my heart unsatisfied.

Oh friend, whose trust I cast aside,
My footsteps falter in my stride;
The memory stings like desert sun,
Reminding me of what's undone.

In every breath, I sense you near,
A hush that beckons me to hear;
Torn by regrets I can't untangle,
My soul remains in silent wrangle.

To love or not, is wisdom's rift,
My fear of wrongness stalls the gift;
I'd cradle your heart if I could,
If only trust were understood.

So here I stand, in sand so still,
My longing echoes in the chill;
I pray to heal this parted scar,
That once was close yet now so far.

BALLAD OF THE BROKEN BRIG

Across a battered deck I pace at dawn,
My mind adrift, my heart half-gone.
She was a brig with sails so torn,
Yet in her wreck, a hope was born.

Her timbers groaned a mournful plea,
Inviting me to set her free.
In every plank, my own faults shone,
Reflections of the trust I'd blown.

Our talk of "eggs" in moonlit cars
Foretold the depth of hidden scars.
I vowed to keep her fragile gift,
But fear's own tempest caused a shift.

In twilight's arms we drifted free,
Where waves of longing met the sea.
Yet when the tide withdrew from sight,
I sank beneath my dread of light.

To right her mast, I gave my all,
But storms within still heard the call.
I tried to guide her broken frame,
And realized my soul's the same.

Rejecting bonds, I seized the helm,
Afraid new shores might overwhelm.
Guilt gnawed at me like salted brine,
For leaving her in swirling brine.

Her battered hull, my battered pride—
Both aching for a safer tide.
The paradox of healing her
Demanded truths I failed to stir.

I cut the ropes that bound us both
To spare my core from deeper growth.
In letting go, I also lost
That chance to mend what fear had cost.

Now in the mirror of the sea,
I glimpse the ship she used to be.
She glides upon the waves at night,
A silent call both wrong and right.

We're both adrift, two wounded hearts,
Once joined by trust that now departs.
Though longing tugs me from afar,
Pride holds me captive where we are.

Still, dreams of masts in distant dawn
Remind me all may not be gone.
If courage stirs beneath this tide,
Perhaps one day our paths collide.

A broken brig once touched my soul,
Revealed a love I can't control.
Yet pride and fear have kept me staunch—
Alone I sail, without her launch

LOVE OF LIFE

REVERIE OF THE UNREACHED HAND

Midnight thoughts press against my ribs,
Telling me I've failed again.
I can't shake the voice declaring my unimportance,
Yet I cling to its cold comfort.

Those who compliment my mind seem distant,
As though they talk about a stranger.
They don't know the shadows I harbor,
The secrets of my private defeats.

I push them away, eyes averted,
Lest they see the cracks in my façade.
In the hush of my obsessions,
I forget promises, ignore warmth.

Commitments become fragile illusions—
Like fragile glass I can't bear to hold.
Shame waits at every misstep,
A lurking specter of guilt.

Once a task seizes my mind,
Everything else slips into irrelevance.
I tell myself no one cares—
It's easier than meeting their eyes.

Truth is, they do care.
I just can't swallow that medicine of praise.
My soul shrinks from the idea
That I might be worthy after all.

This is how self-sabotage thrives:
In the silence of doubt,
In the comfort of old wounds,
Feeding the lie that I don't matter.

Yet some part of me suspects a different story,
A gentle voice saying "You do belong."
But the darkness is safer,
At least for now.

COLONNADE OF QUIET REGRETS

My life unfolds as a calculation—
Friendships, obligations, promises—
I reduce them to risk and reward,
Weighing hearts on a hidden scale.

I missed my friend's long-awaited performance,
A night he'd dreamed of for years.
I claimed I had urgent tasks to complete,
But the haunting sting of regret remains.

I tell myself I'll do better next time,
That I'll make room for those who care.
Yet the sum never settles in my favor,
And I repeat the cycle of neglect.

I see the hurt in his eyes—
A small, quiet betrayal.
He wonders if he ever mattered,
While I'm busy insisting I don't matter at all.

Craving company yet pushing it away,
I use their warmth to ward off cold nights.
Then I slip into silence once I'm content,
Leaving them uncertain, quietly wounded.

Does this really maximize anyone's joy?
I trade lasting bonds for momentary ease,
A hollow logic that fractures trust,
Riddling me with guilt in the aftermath.

Regret deepens in midnight reflections,
Each broken promise echoing loud.
Why measure relationships by utility,
When my spirit craves genuine belonging?

In the end, a deeper truth beckons:
Real connection doesn't conform to equations.
I may deny my worth, but others see it—
And through honest care, our value transcends the sum.

EMBERS OF SELF-BETRAYAL AND HOPE

I drown in the swirl of choices made,
My heart weighs heavy, my spirit afraid.
"I don't matter," the lie I keep,
A shield against vows I fail to keep.

I sense the power in each step I take,
Yet pretend my will might surely break.
Freedom seems too large to bear,
So I hide behind a vacant stare.

I ignore the calls of those who care,
Declining invites I cannot dare.
A friend's big day went on without me,
Haunted by guilt I'd rather not see.

When faced with this quiet despair,
I claim I've nothing left to share.
Responsibility looms in the night,
While I shrink, consumed by inner fight.

"I don't matter," I say once more,
Hoping to dull the ache at my core.
But deep inside, a longing grows,
To break free from the walls I chose.

Regret's taste lingers in silent tears,
A testament to buried fears.
Still, the dawn calls forth each day,
Offering hope I'm tempted to betray.

What if each choice reflects my worth,
A call to rise from trembling earth?
Dismissing myself, I dodge the cost,
Yet each missed moment leaves me lost.

In early light, a voice rings clear,
Whispering truths I barely hear.
I have the power to change my song,
Embracing freedom that makes me strong.

FUCK EVERYBODY NOBODY EXISTS

In this lone chamber, my wrath is born,
I greet the dawn with a sharpened scorn.
I stand unyielding in savage might,
Cursing all bonds that fail my sight.

A desert wind howls in my ear,
It carries no solace, nor calm to hear.
I proclaim with sneer and bitter tongue,
"Fuck everybody," forever sung.

Upon this path I tread with pride,
Discarding warmth that others provide.
My verses drip with stinging distrust,
For "nobody exists" in all this dust.

Tempests of thought swirl in my brain,
No gentle harbor can soothe my pain.
I hurl these words like arrows of spite,
Guarding my soul through endless night.

They gather outside with earnest pleas,
Yet I remain deaf to all their keys.
My fortress stands on silent sand,
I spurn each gesture with a steady hand.

Through gloom I wander, gaze austere,
Their outstretched arms I refuse to revere.
Each step resonates with stern decree,
I claim no place in their company.

Lone footsteps echo on desert floor,
I seal my heart behind iron door.
"Fuck everybody," I carve in stone,
So none may breach this realm I own.

My verses are flames that sear this page,
A testament to unquiet rage.
I scorn the comfort that trust might bring,
Preferring the hush of my suffering.

Here in the shadows, illusions fade,
Promises vanish, no debts are paid.
No sunrise breaks my chosen vow,
Nor soft petition can move me now.

They wait with words of sweet appeal,
But I dismiss them—my heart won't heal.
I repeat that "nobody exists,"
A chant too blunt for catalysts.

My pride stands tall yet stained in gloom,
A poet's posture shaped by doom.
No realm of friendship can claim my mind,
I weigh their worth but leave it behind.

So ends this tale with no respite,
My spirit locked in restless night.
No tender solace can cross my gate,
I languish by choice in this broken state.

SEEKERS OF LIGHT

We stood as soldiers of wonder,
the sea to our backs,
the sky before us a wall of clouds.
The monument stood waiting,
its base rooted in earth,
its height reaching into the unknown,
a tower both of steel and of ambition.

The glow erupted —
a sunrise summoned by human hands.
Its roar came not at once,
but like a conqueror delayed by fate:
seven heartbeats,
then the earth shook.
The sound came in waves,
each one louder,
each one stronger,
until the air became solid
and we were pushed,
as if by unseen hands into the arms of awe.

It rose, this monument of flame,
its light a second dawn,
its song a thunderclap of purpose.
The blue flame beneath,
coiled like a serpent,
wove a double helix,
a symbol of precision,
control, perfection.

Do not tell me the sky is a boundary
when our footsteps rest upon the moon!
It is an invitation,
a silent beckoning for those bold enough to answer.
We who once etched our prayers into stone
now carve our will into the infinite.
We build not to reach,
but to belong.

The flame wrote its testament in the air,
and the rocket ascended,
its ascent a declaration,
its trajectory a spear hurled toward infinity.
Through clouds it disappeared,
but its presence remained:
in the trembling earth,
in the ringing air,
in the hearts of those who dared to watch.

Oh humanity,
who said you have stopped building monuments?
Every launch is a tower raised,
every rocket a cathedral of flame.
We have traded stone for steel,
chisels for engines,
yet the soul of creation remains.

Hail to the engineers,
the dreamers,
the visionaries who defy gravity,
who make of the stars our inheritance.
For we are not bound by soil,
nor by the limits of sight.
We journey beyond,
not as dust, but as seekers of light,

Let the skeptics stay behind,
rooted in the sands of doubt.
We who count down to glory,
who feel the earth's tremble
and hear the sky's roar,
know this truth:
the sky is not our limit—it is our stage.

WHERE HUSHED SKIES MOURN

Between the earth and sky I stand,
With calm, inquiring eyes: "How's life?"
My silence asks, a midnight roam,
A haven for your weary strife.

A man arrives with tears unveiled,
His anchor firm, yet spirit frail.
He speaks of nights devoid of stars,
Of fragile hopes that fade to scars.

His tears like pearls adrift at sea,
Fragile gems of raw misery.
I listen as his wounds confess,
A quiet ache he can't repress.

A woman passes, quiet grace,
Her pain reflected on her face.
She yields her storm, so dark and deep,
In trust that I these truths will keep.

Her faith in me, a silent thread,
Soft whispers only midnight's read.
Her trembling voice with hidden fears,
Echoes across uncertain years.

I guard their secrets, candle-bright,
A watchful presence in the night.
Yet every tale leaves ghosts inside,
Until I lose myself in tides.

The smiles I lend begin to ring
Empty, like an unused string.
For each calm word I offer free,
A piece of me slips quietly.

I wonder if this chosen road
Reveals a deeper vow or code,
For cradling burdens not my own
Has blurred the lines I once had known.

Am I a healer or a thief,
Absorbing pain, yet no relief?
Is this the path I must pursue—
To find myself yet lose me too?

Between the earth and sky I stand,
A vessel for the tears of man.
Balancing each gift of care
With the strength I barely spare.

ELEGANCE AT 5 NANOMETERS

In the land of Longhorns, my journey began,
A reluctant scholar, without a grand plan.
Circuits held no magic, no whispered appeal,
Until Apple's marvel turned fiction to real.

In Craig's domain—a mystic's lair—
The M1 was conjured with vision so rare.
Machines came alive in a synchronized spark,
Proof that design can illuminate dark.

Unified memory singing in tune,
A swift, graceful dance upstaging the moon.
A competitor risen to challenge the throne,
Intel and AMD eclipsed and alone.

Countless transistors in perfect accord,
A revolution forged from lines unexplored.
Not just logic or numbers aligned,
But artistry, beauty, and power combined.

For the first time, I felt design
As creation's spark and logic refined.
No longer mere code on a sterile chart,
But an engine of wonder—a poet's art.

Through Craig's ardor, my doubt released,
A new path opened, reluctance ceased.
Now each circuit reads like living verse,
Every gate a line the mind can rehearse.

So Apple's chip became my muse,
A reason to seize what I once did refuse.
And in its glow, ambition took flight,
An engineer's heart awakened that night.

SAPHIRE EMANATION: THE ALCHEMY OF SELF

Father, do you remember the nights I lay awake,
Weighing your words like stones on my chest?

You taught me to expect the worst before dawn broke,
So that the sunrise felt like a lie I could not trust.

From those days onward, I prepared for failure before I began,
Lowering my own bar so that falling would not hurt so much.

I learned self-sabotage as a second language,
Fluent in the dialect of doubt and dismissal.

Then I saw a man named Elon Musk,
Who forged a car company, a spaceship dream, and a brain-chip venture,
All with an unwavering confidence I thought impossible.

When I applied to UT Austin for electrical engineering,
I had already written my rejection letter in my head,
My GPA was below average, my SAT scores likewise unimpressive,
And I thought I was destined for a lesser tier.

But they answered with acceptance,
Drawn in by an essay that glowed with a passion I seldom recognized in myself.

Astonishment curled in my throat;
I told myself it was a fluke,
I coughed up excuses: luck, pity, a clerical error.
That I had slipped through the back door by mistake.

At my first company, I competed with bright computer science graduates,
Landing a software engineering role I never believed I qualified for.

Getting fired was a punch in the gut, but strangely familiar—
A confirmation that my father's harsh prophecies still held weight.

Contracting for a second company, my manager offered me a promotion twice within two months of starting,
But I refused both times, too afraid of a spotlight I felt unworthy to stand in.

Only when others threatened to take that role—
Threatening also my friends' positions—did I accept,
Stepping into leadership more from duty than confidence.

Starting my own company and securing my first client felt like nepotism,
But in truth, I was the best man for the job—
Yet I still whispered, "I got lucky."

A new circle of friends gathered around me,
Praising my authenticity, my joyfulness, my insight,
And I shrank under their kindness, convinced it was hollow.

I felt like a fraud beneath their admiration,
As if I wore a mask they couldn't see through.

But Father, your echoes no longer bind me—I am no longer that child quivering in your looming shadow.

This is my breakthrough:
I see that every success—UT Austin, the companies I worked at, my own company, my friendships—Was not chance, but an earned triumph. I accept them, finally.

THE TIRED WINGS OF EVENING

My vision, my vision, my vision—
A world where the burden of work does not
Crush our spirits before the sun sets.
I picture offices emptying at dusk,
But the hearts returning home not in surrender
To weariness, not collapsing in front of flickering screens,
But beating with enough life left
For laughter, for gentle instruction, for warmth.

I have seen too many men unclasp their ties
And toss them with a sigh, drained
Of the courage to hold their children's dreams.
I have seen mothers, worried and weighed,
Mask their frustrations in half-smiles,
Their voices too tired to read bedtime stories.
Oh, how many young hearts grow up unheld,
Craving the spark of a parent's guiding touch!

Why do our chores devour our daylight
Like a slow, relentless eclipse?
Why must we endure the marathon of five days,
Only to crown it with two fleeting nights,
Unable to gather the scraps of joy scattered
By the demands of Monday to Friday?
My vision, my vision, my vision—
Let it be a gentle sunrise over our routines,
A new path that gifts each soul
The space to love and the time to blossom.

I do not want your life to be a repeated sigh,
Falling with the evening news.
I want you to return home with music in your voice,
Your arms ready to cradle your children's hopes.
We are called to be more than silent cogs;
We are fathers, mothers, dreamers, doers,
Builders of neighborhoods, sustainers of justice.
Let our days feed the fountains of community,
Instead of draining them.

A DEMOCRACY OF LIGHT

My vision, my vision, my vision—
Is a river that quenches thirst
In the land of the exhausted.
I want a world of wide-awake hearts,
Where men and women, strong from rest,
Stride toward the polling stations with conviction.
Not caged by fatigue, not absent in spirit.
To vote is a dance of choice and hope,
Yet how many skip this waltz
Because they're too worn to believe?

When 63.9% cast a ballot,
And those 50-50 lines define our future,
Who speaks for the ones too tired to care,
Too jaded, too pressed by time,
To watch democracy flourish?

What of the absent half that surrenders
To the hush of apathy?
I see them falling asleep at the threshold of change,
Their voices drowned in the hum
Of a daily grind that never ends.

My vision, my vision, my vision—
Grows from the quiet sorrow in my blood.
I have tasted the bitterness of workplaces
That twist honor into monotony,
Leaving families with only worn-out husks.
A father's jokes left unspoken, a mother's lullaby undone,
Communities gasping for volunteers, for neighbors,
For hands that shape the future of our children.
Are we not the architects of tomorrow?
We cannot build if our bodies are broken.

Let us imagine a democracy of light,
In which work exists for life
And not life for work.
Where the flame of engagement is never dimmed
By the bitterness of exhaustion.
In that place, the smallest voice matters,
And the largest heart thrives,
And from that place, we rise together,
To choose not only our leaders,
But our shared destiny.

IN THE SHADOW OF PARENTS

My vision, my vision, my vision—
A song weaving through my childhood nights,
Echoing in the hush of weary footsteps.
I watched my parents return home,
Their eyes clouded with a day's worth of heartache,
Their smiles flickering, tested by toxic demands.
I saw the cost of survival etched
In their trembling hands.

How many birthdays pass in half-celebrations
Because mothers and fathers are hostage
To the next urgent deadline,
The unyielding phone calls,
The mountain of tasks that never truly end?
How many community halls wait dim and empty,
While we collapse, each alone,
In the prison of exhaustion?

Yet hope grows from the cracks in the pavement:
The promise that tomorrow can bloom differently,
That workplaces can be gardens, not factories,
That we might come home
With hearts still ablaze, ready to nurture.
I speak for the child who grew up watching
The toll of a suffocating job on the ones who loved him,
And I vow to end that cycle of quiet sorrow.

My vision, my vision, my vision—
It stands as a sentinel over every cubicle,
A bright lamp in each break room,
Insisting that the day's labor
Must not rob us of our night's joy.
No father should have to choose
Between a steady paycheck and an honest presence,
No mother should be forced to trade
Her child's laughter for overtime's hollow coin.

CIGARETTES IN THE RAIN: A MIDNGIHT MEMOIR

I sometimes think of these nights as my personal epic poems—just written in neon instead of ink.

It was Valentine's Day, one of those singles' gatherings where everyone pretends they aren't lonely. When I got there, the mood was...fine. Fine in the sense that everyone was going through the motions: awkward flirting, half-laughs at each other's jokes, "cards-against-humanity-before-dating" or something like that. I was already exhausted from a workout that left me stuttering, which tends to happen when I'm dead tired. The whole setup felt forced.

A cluster of folks decided to head to an EDM show at The Concourse. I started out with a plan of my own—two-stepping at White Horse with a girl who seemed nice enough. But first, she needed to drop off some stuff at her place. Outside her house, it rained. I leaned on my car, smoked two slow cigarettes, and let raindrops keep time on my shoulders. She took forever to come out and I was almost ready to leave without her. Right when I was about to bail, she appeared. No apology, just "Let's go."

We hit the road. My phone buzzed. It was my friend from the gathering: he was doing mushrooms and about to see BAYNK. He said I had to join. At this point I didn't really want to dance with her. I looked at the girl. She shrugged and said, Sure, why not? I told her I might not be able to drive her home—that she'd have to Uber or hitch a ride back with somebody else. She was cool with it. Right then, I knew the evening was taking a sharp left turn.

The Concourse

I handed over my forty bucks for the ticket. The girl sighed dramatically and claimed she forgot her wallet. Her Apple Pay didn't work... apparently. Sigh. Another $40. I already felt a twinge of regret. This is not my lady of the night, I decided. I did not want to drive her all the way back or leave her out in the cold. She was my responsibility, at least until we parted ways.

Inside, lights strobing, bodies pressed against each other in ecstatic motion. My friends were already floating on a mushroom cloud. They waved me over, handed me one, told me to settle in. An hour passed. Nothing. So I took a second. Still nothing.

But mushrooms have a way of sneaking up on you. Suddenly, that warm tingalinaling sensation bloomed in my calves like champagne bubbles. By the time it reached my thighs, my torso, my lungs—my esophagus, of all places—I was in another dimension. It felt like music was breathing me instead of the other way around. I brushed past strangers, feeling elegantly smooth, drifting from my group to other corners, swaying with new faces. I laughed when I spotted a guy in a wiZard costume earlier; now, I set on a quest to find him.

When I headed outside to the courtyard for some air and to share a cigarette with a gorgeous stranger, there he was, as if conjured: the wiZard, perched near the exit. I felt like I'd discovered buried treasure. Right after sharing a cigarette with a gorgeous stranger, I ran after him and asked the wiZard for a picture. He obliged. Through my mushroom haze, I believed we'd formed some cosmic bond.

The Afterparty

BAYNK ended, lights came up. My friends huddled around, deciding what to do next. They wanted to crash, but I needed more. So did they, maybe, but they were fighting sleep. I told them I was hitting an after-party and they could come if they wanted. Eventually, I ventured out alone.

I drove out to 6th street. Found a place with no sign, no windows, just a blank door with a CCTV camera perched above it. I flashed my QR code like a half-hearted spy. Knocked. No response. I sighed, about to give up, when a group of girls tumbled out, giggling, and left the door swinging open long enough for me to slip in.

Inside, the scene was pure excess: men in leopard-print leggings that left nothing to the imagination, fur coats with huge collars, platform boots, couples making out in corners or vanishing behind curtains, re-emerging with jackets askew. At the bar, people ordered drinks even though we were way past last call. The bathrooms were… occupied. I saw Skyn lube packets strewn across the sinks, two people stumbling out of a stall. I wondered what kind of membership card you need to feel normal here.

I ordered a rum and Coke. It felt bizarre to be the only one at the bar with wide eyes, a little too aware of how out-of-place I looked. Then I saw this giant of a man—six-foot-five—wearing a sumptuous coat and a gold chain with three pendants. The middle pendant was bigger, an obvious focal point. I couldn't help it; I walked up and complimented him and his high-waisted pants. Turned out his name was Darius. He had that snap in his voice that told me he was proud of his flamboyance. Our laughter and easy smiles drew more people in, and soon I was folded into their circle. This was definitely not an office crowd.

We all tried to leave for another party, but it was like herding cats in outer space. One person would wander off; we'd go to retrieve them, then another would vanish. Finally, Darius and I wound up outside in a cold, wet alley, locked out. We laughed at the absurdity. Eventually, the rest of them found us.

The Electric Church

We ended up at a place called the Electric Church—some kind of makeshift venue in East Austin that's half religious tribute, half psychedelic art trap house. Foil on the ceilings, random graffiti, gift wrap on walls, random photos plastered on the walls. It stank of spilled beer and the hum of a hundred people brushing shoulders.

We made our way through one dim-lit room after another until we found a tiny back room—karaoke. In that 10-by-10 space, a sofa lined the wall, and a small TV flickered in the corner like it might cut out any second. The glow of Chinese lanterns bobbed overhead.

People sang eighties hits: "Me and Michael," "Eyes Without a Face." Then Darius stepped up for "Smooth Operator," swaying his hips with relish. He crooned into the mic like a lounge singer. It fit him too well. Finally, someone pointed to me: "Your turn." I picked "American Idiot," a jarring choice after all the silky pop. I gave my phone to some drunk guy on the floor, hoping he could record a video. He was so wasted I suspected half the footage would be of the ceiling.

But I didn't care. I poured everything out: "DON'T WANNA BE AN AMERICAN IDIOT!" I banged my head 'till I broke my neck. The crowd roared. My mind rode the wave of mushrooms and uncountable drinks. By the end, I was drenched in sweat.

Then came the flashing lights—red and blue lights. Cops. It was 4 AM, time to shut it down. Everyone filed out calmly. On our way out, we ran into someone named Ooga—the organizer. He told us to wait. That's how we met a man who was hopelessly drunk, let's call him C, who invited us back to his place. The night had no bottom.

Rainey Street

Rainey Street, an empty apartment with a single couch, a TV propped on stools, a Playstation blinking in the corner, and a massive brown bookshelf stacked with art. C had a "plug" who delivered White Claws and lemon tequila. One of the guys pulled out a couple bags of coke. We passed them around, chasing them with gulps of cheap alcohol, exhaling in half-laughter, half-disbelief.

We talked about everything—fashion, health insurance, poems. At some point, a girl and I slipped out to the balcony where I recited "Halos of Metal at the Witching Hour." But the others followed, curious, and I performed for everyone, heart pounding, eyes half-closed.

Morning Light

By 7 AM, we'd run out of everything except for small talk. The sky hinted at dawn. I remembered my Saturday Tradition workout at 7:30. I never miss it. Not for a holiday, not for a hangover. I said my goodbyes and headed to the gym. I might've been delirious and reeked of sweat and stale liquor, but I was there and finished every set.

Soon after that and breakfast with the boys, I was out driving 45 minutes to a baby shower in Dripping Springs, TX past rolling hills, brightening sky, the city behind me. The contrast was almost poetic—celebrating new life while my brain was still swirling from a night that had zero boundaries. If someone had told me I'd be standing in a pastel-decorated club house, feet sore from dancing, mind drifting back to a wiZard in VIP and a 6'5 fashion king belting out Sade, I might've laughed. But that's how Valentine's night bled into morning.

I guess some stores are open all night. And sometimes, if you're lucky—or unlucky—you walk in and realize you don't care how long you stay.

AFTERWORD

On Sunday, February 2, 2025, I devoted thirteen uninterrupted hours to meticulously refining this book—polishing every one of the last 130 pages. All that remained was a final flourish: page numbering, a few subtle layout adjustments, and then uploading it to Amazon. I was so close, I could practically taste that moment of triumph—like that sharp rush you get when your boots finally click into the stirrups. By 2 a.m., I decided I'd done enough for one night.

The next morning, I checked my schedule and realized it would be another week before I'd have time to work on the book again. That's when the thought hit: *Why the fuck am I even doing this?* I'm already near the finish line—why cross it? Why not walk away? Truth is, I've seen myself do this before: get close to completion, pivot, and leave behind a string of half-finished projects. But clearly, here we are, and you're holding the proof in your hands—so this time, I made sure I finished the job.

STRINGS OF TWILIGHT: A PERSONAL CURATION

I.	"100" – Dean Blunt
II.	"You're All I Want" – Cigarettes After Sex
III.	"505" – Arctic Monkeys
IV.	"The Adults are Talking" – The Strokes
V.	"Notion" – The Rare Occasions
VI.	"Facebook.com" – Memo Boy
VII.	"The Void Stares Back" – WARGASM
VIII.	"Do It So Good" – WARGASM
IX.	"Scratchcard Feeling" – WARGASM
X.	"PYRO PYRO" – WARGASM
XI.	"Heaven Knows I'm Miserable Now" – The Smiths
XII.	"They're Hanging Me Tonight" – Marty Robbins
XIII.	"El Paso" – Mart Robbins
XIV.	"Nobody Knows My Trouble" – Ryan Bingham
XV.	"No Horse To Ride" – Luke Grimes
XVI.	"Take This Job and Shove It" – Johnny Paycheck
XVII.	"Feathered Indians" – Tyler Childers

ABOUT THE AUTHOR

I fuse an engineer's precision with a poet's heart, bridging the worlds of function and artistry. Growing up between Arab and Texan cultures, I found inspiration in Islamic geometry—the very motif that graces my book's cover. Riding English taught me that leadership is a subtle language of gentle tugs and nudges, a skill I carried into two-stepping. Dance began as a quest to communicate with elegance and became a pursuit of genuine connection.

Women are works of art, and that's how I treat them. Whether I'm refining code, guiding a horse, or gliding across the dance floor, I believe in the power of nuanced expression. In every act—be it welding steel, composing verse, or building bridges between two rich cultures—I strive for the same quiet finesse that turns effort into an art form.

CONNECT

For personal or literary inquiries:
@ennismsalam on all major platforms
salam@ennismsalam.com

For business or AI consulting:
ShieldStone Labs – My AI consulting company
salam@shieldstonelabs.com
shieldstonelabs.com

Made in the USA
Columbia, SC
19 March 2025